Building the Bridge Inward through Meditation

A guide to the doorway of Divine direction and connection

Lynzie Bailey

Master your inner home, so your outer world reflects the transformation.

Author's Tranquility Press
MARIETTA, GEORGIA

Copyright © 2022 by Lynzie Bailey.

All rights reserved. No part of this publication may be reproduced, distributed or transmitted in any form or by any means, including photocopying, recording, or other electronic or mechanical methods, without the prior written permission of the publisher, except in the case of brief quotations embodied in critical reviews and certain other noncommercial uses permitted by copyright law. For permission requests, write to the publisher, addressed "Attention: Permissions Coordinator," at the address below.

Lynzie Bailey/Author's Tranquility Press
2706 Station Club Drive SW
Marietta, GA 30060
www.authorstranquilitypress.com

Ordering Information:
Quantity sales. Special discounts are available on quantity purchases by corporations, associations, and others. For details, contact the "Special Sales Department" at the address above.

Building the Bridge Inward through Meditation/Lynzie Bailey
Paperback: 978-1-957546-73-5
eBook: 978-1-957546-74-2

Acknowledgments

To my Angels and Guides: Thank you for your trust in me to co-create this program and for your support as I continue on my spiritual journey.

To my talented writing coach, Sue, for her openness and trust in the creative process.

To Kyle Devine and Chris Rubeo for their sound design, creative composition, and incredible patience.

To Victoria for her gracious gift that has allowed me to republish this meditation guide almost five years after its initial publication. Victoria, I am so grateful for your generosity and giving spirit. You have made it possible for this guide to reach a wider audience at the very moment it is most needed...timing is everything!

I am eternally grateful for all those who have supported me in my evolution and spiritual growth.

There are no shortcuts to enlightenment; you must live it to be it! Lynzie Bailey

Contents

Part I: Introduction to Building the Bridge Inward through Meditation: A guide to the doorway of Divine direction and connection 1

Part II: Getting Started on Connecting with Your Higher Self 5

Part III: Bonus Meditation — Centering and Aligning Your Energy 10

Part IV: Higher Guidance Meditations 1 – 5 11

Part V: Mental Check-In 13

Part VI: Higher Guidance Meditations 6 – 8 15

Part VII: Higher Guidance Meditations 9 and 10 16

Part VIII: An Invitation from Lynzie 17

Part IX: Inspirations and Insights Journal 19

About the Author 34

With the purchase of this guide, you receive access to the audio files of the meditations at no extra cost. To download the audio files, you can either scan the QR code or type the website link below into your web browser and follow the instructions:

https://www.thebridgeinward.com/meditation-guide-downloads/

Part I: Introduction to Building the Bridge Inward through Meditation: A guide to the doorway of Divine direction and connection

Meditation is a way to give your brain a chance to slow-way-down and allow for the space to simply BE. It is the same concept as going to sleep to give your body time to recover from the stress of your day.

When you sleep, your breathing slows, your muscles relax, tissue growth and repair occurs, and your energy is restored. Sleep helps you to thrive by contributing to a healthy immune system.

Meditating gives your brain time to recuperate just as sleep helps your body recover. Meditation has other benefits as well, such as significant brain wave activity, namely increased Theta and Alpha, which are associated with wakeful and relaxed attention. Meditation is also calming to the central nervous system and can benefit those who suffer from hypertension, anxiety, and depression.

It is disheartening that we as a society have been conditioned to believe that, if we aren't always doing, multitasking, or taking care of someone else's needs first before our own, we are less valuable. That "doing" defines our value as a human being. My experience tells me that we are all Human Beings who do not always have to be Humans Doing.

One of the biggest stumbling blocks to starting and maintaining a meditation practice can be the ability to relax, let go, and be fully present for 10 or more minutes without checking out mentally or falling asleep. Giving yourself permission to relax so that you are able to meditate can bring up all kinds of anxiety around self-judgment, -criticism and -worth.

I still sometimes struggle with being present in the moment during my daily meditation, so I understand the challenges the process presents to those who undertake it. Let my program be your opportunity to create the time, space, and attention necessary to beginning and maintaining a practice of your own. If you stick with it, the benefits 100-percent-outweigh the challenges you will face as you begin.

Meditation is not only a way to quiet and calm yourself but a way to receive higher guidance, which I like to refer to as "your own personal inner navigation system". This guidance comes from your infinite connection to the Divine, also known as your higher self.

We all have Spirit Guides, Angels, and Helpers who are assigned to us from the beginning of our existence. They watch over us 24 / 7 and are always there to assist us whenever we reach out for help. Because we have free will here on earth, the Spirit Guides and Angels cannot interfere without being asked – so ask when you need guidance. And then get quiet, be open and willing to listen to what may come through.

You may not be aware of these beings unless you make getting to know them a part of your conscious awareness. If this terminology does not fit into your particular belief system, you may simply call this being "God", "Buddha", "Jesus", "Spirit", or whatever you are most comfortable with. This practice is your unique and very personal relationship with the Divine designed by you to fit you. I will refer to the beings as the Divine, Spirit, Soul, or Higher Self to make the meditations simple to follow.

Once you have settled into a regular practice and are able to sit quietly without racing thoughts, you can actually make a game of it. An example of this is asking your higher self or Spirit for a symbol or sign to watch out for on a daily basis. I would suggest doing this as you start to establish your connection with this being, and you have the hang of it.

As you see more signs that your Angels and Guides are near, express your gratitude as a way to confirm that you are being accompanied on your life's journey. I do this regularly and when I see these symbols, or experience synchronistic events, I like to write about them in my journal, in my blog, or in other writing. You can decide for yourself how you want to express these building blocks of faith.

Your first step in getting started is to create a connection with that special being. You may want to name the being(s) or you may intuit a name; however, I will preface each meditation with a direction that you call forth only the "Beings of the highest light and vibration who are a part of your Spirit Family" for your protection. I would encourage you to do this each time you meditate. (Refer to the recording of the bonus meditation for a grounding and protection exercise.)

Once you have established a regular meditation practice and are able to bring yourself into your center fairly easily, the next step is to get into the habit of making the connection. You

will want to get a feel for this being's or these beings' energy and the way in which you receive your guidance.
Do you receive messages through vision or seeing (also known as clairvoyance), do you hear messages (also known as clairaudience), or do you feel them (which is known as clairsentience)? You can even have a combination of two or more types of connection to the Spirit world.

The point is that we all experience truth differently. But we will know it as truth and as supportive of our and the world's best interest in our very core (our gut, you might say) no matter how it comes to us – visually, auditorily or tactically. On the other side of the coin of truth, we sense the poison of a lie in a similar fashion.

As you start to receive guidance, you will soon learn to trust and have faith that the first thing that pops into your head or that you hear, see, or feel in your heart is your answer. Remaining open and without attachment or judgment is a good place to start because sometimes you may not get the answer or answers you want. However, the answers you do receive will always be for your highest good and the good of all concerned.

Part II: Getting Started on Connecting with Your Higher Self

The goal of this program is to enable you to clear the mind chatter and nervous energy that can cloud your thinking – interrupting your chance to even notice if information is coming through. Once you have trained yourself to sink into that quiet space, you will then be able to ask questions and receive answers concerning any challenging circumstance or circumstances you may be facing, as well as any and every aspect of your life.

If you have never meditated before, go into this with the understanding that you will want to make a firm commitment and have patience with yourself and not be hard on yourself. This process takes time, effort, and the will to learn to stay with the practice, even on days when you are most challenged to stick with it. Once you make the commitment to yourself, it will become easier. You can liken it to playing an instrument. Unless you're a prodigy, in order to sharpen your skills, you must practice.

I understand how challenging meditating can be, and I can honestly say that I am not always able to clear my own mind chatter or feel completely free of anxiety going into a meditation. We all have busy lives and sometimes it is hard to let go, and that's okay. I've put this program together to share some of the epiphanies I have had, as well as some of my own struggles. We are all here on planet earth to evolve and grow, and we don't do either without experiencing challenges. Neither do we overcome the challenges without help and support from others.

I would suggest setting aside a minimum of 20 to 30 minutes every morning for your meditation. You can do this in the afternoon or evening if that time works best for you; however, you don't want to meditate when you are sleepy, if you can help it, such as right after lunch or before bed. The intention is to quiet your mind of all thoughts to the best of your ability. Don't beat yourself up if you just can't quiet your mind. Go ahead and do the meditation anyway. Taking time to focus inwardly without interruption is most important and will strengthen your meditation muscle.

When your mind is quiet, you can start to see, feel, or sense things you may not have noticed before. You may feel sensations in your body, and / or an overwhelming grief or joy may surface. You are connecting with another sense you may not have known you had. Meditation is experiential; you must experience it to know how it feels for you. Find your rhythm, and you will reap great rewards that will help you in all aspects of your life.

Journaling is very important to help you remember your experience more vividly. This is the time when creative projects and solutions to problems you have been struggling with come through. Journaling is also a way to track your progress as you go more deeply into your meditation practice.

Also, be aware that you may not receive messages that are in plain English or provided linearly. As I mentioned previously, you may see a picture, a single word, or a short phrase, or you may have a sensation of strong feeling in your body as a "knowing". Sometimes you may not get anything at all.

Don't try to force it; this may be a time of simple reflection and the answers may come later. I have experienced countless meditations where I just sat in silence and simply enjoyed the high vibrational loving energy streaming through and all around me. Know that you are still reaping the rewards of the practice of quieting your mind, and that every time you do this, your skills improve and your connection to the Divine is strengthened.

Stay open and pay attention – especially when you're in nature. This is a place signs and / or answers may show up. Watch for repeating numbers and synchronistic events; these, too, are ways to receive communication. When you meditate, you are showing the Universe and your Angels and Guides that you are open to their communications, so they will start showing up everywhere. Know that you are being guided and remain open to the boundless support that is all around you – always.

I recommend setting an intention before you begin your meditation. If you are having a particular problem or challenge that you need specific help with, get clear about what it is and say a short prayer before your meditation. You could also write it out in your journal, following it up by recording any answers below the original entry. You could also stay in your meditative state after you have finished doing the meditation so that you can ask additional questions.

Suggestions from Lynzie for getting your meditation session off to a good start

If possible, make sure you have a place to meditate where you won't be disturbed. I like to wear headphones because this helps me keep my focus and also drowns out any background noise.

If you can dim the lights and / or close the drapes or blinds, this too can help you stay focused. You'll also want to keep your back straight to allow the energy to move freely through your spine. It's also best to have your feet flat on the floor; however, you might want to lie down. Just make sure you are comfortable before you begin.

If you'd like, light a candle or some incense. If you are into crystals and want to hold a crystal or place one on a part of your body – this, too, is perfectly appropriate. If you prefer to meditate in nature, or you have to perform your meditation in your car, no problem. If noise and light don't bother you, it's not necessary to wear headphones or dim the lights. Set up your meditation space the way it works best for you.

The last thing I want to offer to you is the option of doing a grounding exercise before each meditation, especially as you begin setting up and establishing your practice. This exercise will help you feel more connected, not only during the meditation itself, but also afterwards to help you feel this way throughout your day. Additionally, this grounding meditation can be done any time you feel the world around you is spinning, or you simply want to feel centered and balanced. It's also a great way to begin your day.

Included in the grounding bonus meditation, I also offer a set of instructions on how to protect your energy field from merging with others or vice versa. The grounding exercise keeps you protected from unwanted energy not part of your Spirit family.

Once you have the grounding exercise down, you can do this exercise anywhere, any time. This bonus meditation is short and sweet and can only enhance what you are creating in your daily practice and your life.

An important last step to every meditation is to drink water. Hydrating yourself helps you move any stagnant energy out of the body. A walk in nature after an especially intense meditation session can also help release negative energy that may have been dislodged.

Finally, I would suggest that you get your space ready and yourself comfortable before starting your meditation. This way you won't miss any part of the recording, nor will you have to pause the recording to make these adjustments. However, if you are having difficulty relaxing yourself, then go ahead, pause, breathe, and start again.

You design your meditation environment with what is most appropriate and feels most natural for YOU! Remember: This is your practice to design the way you want so that it fits your schedule and your life. There are no hard or fast rules.

Now relax and enjoy the exploration!

Part III: Bonus Meditation — Centering and Aligning Your Energy

Doing this grounding exercise can only enhance your feeling of connection between you and your Divine Creator because it functions as a kind of umbilical cord from earth through you to your Source. The bonus meditation can also be done by itself when you don't have the time to dedicate to a full meditation. This process can be repeated in just a few short minutes any time during the day, especially when you feel scattered and want to regain your balance and inner peace.

The grounding exercise is also a way to help keep you protected from darker energies that can penetrate you, instigating a fear reaction that can make you weak and vulnerable. If you know you are going to be in a situation where your energy will be challenged, such as crowded events, restaurants, or stores, I highly recommend doing this exercise before and after the activity.

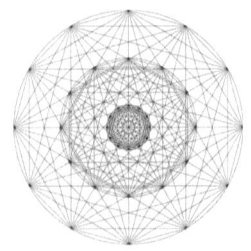

Part IV: Higher Guidance Meditations 1 – 5

Meditation has helped me create a connection with my Higher Self, the Universe, and the Divine. This connection, in turn, has drawn to me, as if I were a magnet, a whole community of like-minded people. I now have an entire Universe surrounding me with Love and Support in all aspects of my life. In writing and recording these meditations for you, I hope to show YOU how it's possible to accomplish this in your own life.

Meditation is a practice, which means that, with practice, you will be able to become more focused in all that you do, whether you are meditating or living your life. Twenty minutes may seem like an eternity when you're first starting out; however, as time goes on and as you hang in there through your struggles and not give up, your skills will improve, and the Cosmos will soon become your playground.

These meditations all come from my own personal experience, and I use them in my work and my personal life. In each of the first few meditations I include steps for you to prepare for the session by getting comfortable in a setting that is conducive to meditation. You may not always have this option, so just do the best you can. These preparation steps help you establish a routine for the sessions that will become second nature soon enough.

I recommend that you keep a meditation journal, and if you have a few moments after a meditation session or during your day, jot down any insights or aha's. This is the time when the creative juices flow and the best time to receive insights and guidance, so pay attention! You may also notice your dreams becoming more animated and meaningful than before, so keep a pen and paper on your nightstand to jot down anything unusual that comes through.

Are you excited to start this journey with me? I am!

I recommend that you keep a meditation journal.

Part V: Mental Check-In

We all have good days and days that are more challenging or simply downright painful. As I mentioned previously, meditation is just the right method to use to seek inner balance and peace – especially on the rough days. But I also know that these times offer the biggest challenges to our ability to focus and not be derailed by our ego, our inner critic – the one who expects perfection to the detriment of our taking time to connect within.

Wherever you are in the program, this may be a good time to do a mental check-in and ask yourself the following questions:

- Am I staying on track with my meditation practice?
- Have I been diligent about setting aside time to meditate every day?
- Am I progressing in my meditation practice?
- Am I enjoying my meditation practice?

Sometimes we can get off track. Life happens, and we can lose our focus, our momentum, and that's okay! Now is the time to regain your focus, set a new goal, and keep moving forward.

Don't worry if you've been led astray or have given up – those are only temporary frames of mind.

You can start again.

Each time you push past your self-placed limitations, you grow in your faith. Know that wherever you are, I am with you, supporting you in achieving your greatest success on this journey. It's important to me that you succeed. When you succeed, I do too.

Part VI: Higher Guidance Meditations 6 – 8

As you progress through meditations 6 to 8, the meditations lengthen, with more time during the pauses. This is to encourage you to stretch yourself, extending the time you spend reflecting inward. Consider this your growth period and that sometimes growth and change can be uncomfortable. Stay with any feelings that surface; don't push them down or deny them. Those feelings are a part of you that is being brought to the surface and into the light.

Think of negative feelings as sediment at the bottom of your oil pan. When your oil gets stirred up, this sediment can come to the surface. You don't want this sludge settling back in; you want it to be released. This is key to your moving those lower vibration energies out and making room for more Divine light. Be with the discomfort, and it will eventually dissipate. If you are willing to face this fear, you will love the transformation that will occur.

Continue journaling because this will help you see patterns that may be forming and reveal the real and true you beneath your outer persona. If you are consistent, this process will elicit aha's.

Part VII: Higher Guidance Meditations 9 and 10

You are now rounding the bend to the advanced portion of this program. Take a moment to reflect back on how far you have come. Celebrate yourself for sticking with it, even if you've had some difficulty with emotions and / or anxiety. Remember: Working through your fears and eliminating any blocks that seem to hold you back is how you stretch and grow.

If you ever feel you need to drop back and return to any of the previous meditations, do so. They can serve as a reminder of how far you have progressed. I have said this before: This is your very own personal practice to discover the ways that work best for you. Move forward with confidence, a new awareness and inner strength that will support you on many different levels. Now enjoy the last two meditations, and I will look forward to hearing your reactions in a testimonial. Here's the link to my Contact page:
https://thebridgeinward.com/contact-lynzie/.

And here's a link to my blog to share your thoughts on what I've written: https://www.TheBridgeInward.com/blog.

Part VIII: An Invitation from Lynzie

First and foremost, I ask that you acknowledge yourself for how far you have come in your practice by looking back for just a moment – so you can look forward with a new confidence you didn't have before you began this program.

Secondly, I offer up this question for you to ponder, "Where does this leave me?"

I don't see this as the end of the road of meditating or creating – for you or for me. My dream, when I first began this work, was to facilitate the creation of a like-minded community of people all over the world who answer the call of their soul's urgings. I consider you, dear reader, a part of that community because you have purchased this meditation guide. And, of course, you can always share your thoughts regarding my blog articles and other writings. Go to my blog at: https://www.thebridgeinward.com/blog/ so that you can read my latest article, which includes real-life stories and tips on how to live a life motivated by a higher purpose.

Stay committed to improving your meditation skills. Stay connected to your inner home, and any time you have a decision to make, seek your answers within.

I thank you sincerely for sharing with me in this experience of growth and transcendence as, together, we continue on our journey.

In the spirit of continuous learning, I ask that you type or record a short video testimonial of your experience while using this program. Please attach the audio file to an email message (or type your message into the body of the email) and send it to lynziebailey@thebridgeinward.com . Put "Testimonial" in the subject line. And if you feel comfortable sending a photograph of yourself along with your testimonial, I would love to have it on my site.

Your insights will help me to change what isn't working and add important content to future programs, mentoring sessions, publications, and blog articles.

Part IX: Inspirations and Insights Journal

I have mentioned throughout this program that journaling is a way to connect the dots. It's how you can record anything that comes through your meditations – especially things that seem like minute details but can be the golden thread that binds your life experiences together in ways you may never have imagined before.

The Higher Realms are always communicating with us. However, too much of the time, we are too preoccupied to hear over the noise of life. Chasing kids, dealing with teens' school projects and assignments, working outside the home, doing housework and laundry, tracking finances, caring for elderly parents, dealing with the intricacies of electronics, and more...These things can all limit the time you have to spend on your meditation practice.

Take this meditation time you have and use every moment to glean information pertinent to finding your way to your best Divine path. Use your journal as a springboard to take your consciousness to a deeper level. Understand why you are here and the gift that you are and that you are meant to share.

If you think of your meditation practice and journaling as a way to recharge your personal battery and energize your connection with Mother Earth and the Divine, you can see it as a vital component of self-care – like eating healthy foods, exercising, and brushing your teeth. Maintaining your spiritual health is just as important to your personal growth and development as paying attention to your mental and physical well-being. You are made of mind, body, and spirit, and they all need to function in an integrated manner for you to be your best self.

The journal included at the end of this guide is my gift to you so that you can begin to document your meditation journey as it unfolds. Almost from the beginning of my meditation practice, I kept a journal. I wrote things down I felt were important and even things I wasn't sure were significant, but later turned out to be.

As I developed my communications with the Spirit world, I journaled about my emotions, symbolic things showing up in nature, people I was running into, my dreams and my awareness of myself and how I related to others. Suddenly, I was noticing details I had been used to ignoring. My life was instantly more in focus and "in color".

I share these details with you today because of how they have affected my life with such significance that it changed the direction 100 percent. Now, I can tell you that I have a very strong connection with my intuition, my Angels and Guides. I live my life by my guidance. I ask about everything.

At times, I may have been guided into situations I did not expect to be in, but those situations always contributed to a deepening of my faith and the development of my character, internal strength, and courage. For perhaps the first time in my life, I found myself stepping over the boundaries I had created for myself – the ones that told me "You can't do that." or "That's too hard." I pushed open the doors of my fear and found opportunities instead of disaster.

I want this for you! Even if you only write two words, write them!! You may look back someday, and those two words could change everything.

Track your progress and see how far you've come, how much you've learned, how you've opened yourself up to the "SOUL you". Remove the projections of others, their limiting beliefs that have influenced you so strongly. Find your own truth and sing your own song!

Happy journaling!

Inspirations and Insights

Inspirations and Insights

Inspirations and Insights

Inspirations and Insights

Inspirations and Insights

Inspirations and Insights

Inspirations and Insights

Inspirations and Insights

Inspirations and Insights

Inspirations and Insights

Inspirations and Insights

Inspirations and Insights

About the Author

Lynzie Bailey grew up the middle child in a family of seven. Religion dominated the family dynamic, as did her parents' upbringing during the depression and World War II.

Until the age of 50, Lynzie believed that a ceiling and walls caged her world and that she could go only so far until...choosing to let go of her physical home precipitated a Spiritual Awakening, revealing that she had a choice about her spiritual home as well. Her inner home's boundaries disappeared, and her spirit was freed.

Lynzie's meditation guide was born out of experience with developing her meditation practice. In the guide, she invites readers to come on a journey to discover their Divine connection. Her meditation guide is for those with a deep spiritual hunger to connect with their soul. She is now gathering a community of individuals to whom she says, "As I have done, so you can, too.

www.ingramcontent.com/pod-product-compliance
Lightning Source LLC
LaVergne TN
LVHW040203080526
838202LV00042B/3296